FORD
T-BirD

FORD
T-BirD

Malcolm Birkitt

First published in 1992 by
Osprey Publishing Limited
59 Grosvenor Street London W1X 9DA

Cataloguing in Publication Data for this title
is available from the British Library.

ISBN 1 85532 214 5

Editor Shaun Barrington
Page design Angela Posen
Printed in Hong Kong

Front cover
*Was there a better sight and sound on
American highways in the 1960s than
a bright red Thunderbird convertible
cruising along, its V-8 motor gently
making music? Many classic T-Bird
owners would say no, and still feel the
same way three decades later*

Half-title page
*Though Ford chose to call the
Thunderbird a personal and not a
sports car, the 1955 model carried
these chequered flags on the bonnet
and boot as a sign of its performance
potential. Some cars were used in road
racing, but with moderate success. In
1957, a short run of roadgoing
supercharged Littlebirds was
produced, developing some 300 bhp
and giving some really impressive
straight-line speed*

Title-page
*Ride quality in a straight line was a
Squarebird plus. Steering, though
light, was too slow and even moderate
cornering induced plenty of body lean*

Right
*Class Act – that's what the owners of
this '65 convertible think of their
restored T-Bird*

For a catalogue of all books published by Osprey Automotive
please write to:

**The Marketing Department, Octopus Illustrated Books,
1st Floor, Michelin House, 81 Fulham Road, London SW3 6RB**

Contents

Introduction

All kinds of four wheelers have been embraced during the course of America's long love affair with the automobile. But few have penetrated the heart as deeply as has Ford's Thunderbird. Today, it must rank among the most durable names in US automotive history. Because remarkably, there's still a car rolling off an assembly line bearing the familiar blue oval badge and the emotive 'Thunderbird' title, more than thirty-five years after the first T-bird made its public début.

Though the T-Bird has been part of the American landscape for around four decades, it is the earliest years of production which have created the most interest. These cars have come to symbolise the American Dream. How else do you explain the number of pop songs which refer to the car in their lyrics? During the early Sixties, for instance, the Beach Boys surfed into town singing 'She'll have fun, fun, fun 'til her Daddy takes the T'Bird away.' Two decades later Prince, from the motor city of Detroit himself, crooned away on Alphabet Street, 'I'm gonna drive my Daddy's Thunderbird...'.

Now classic Thunderbirds take part in promotional videos, rest

high above our heads on display plinths above cafés, appear in signs for various eateries, and remain the pride and joy of numerous private owners. Without question, the **T-Bird** image is intact and firmly embedded in **US** popular culture.

After a period in the doldrums, the Thunderbird is once more a fine, dynamic motor car. But most believe Ford's genuinely golden era of production occurred between 1955 and 1966. In that relatively short period three clearly discernible generations of car were made, sharing little but two doors apiece and a growing taste for luxury. The cars are affectionately known as Littlebird, Squarebird and Bigbird respectively. Each version was, and still is, dearly loved. Those dozen years and these classic models are the precise scope of this book.

Though one author's name appears on the cover, books of this nature are really a result of the efforts of many people. Some individuals provided information or pictures, while others contributed that invaluable commodity – inspiration! All were generous with their help, and have probably forgotten more about classic Thunderbirds than I'll ever know. My thanks then to:

Jack Barnes, John Cox, Bob Gadra, Lance Herrington, Lucky Roberts, Robert and Pat Smith, Mike Stanley, Don and Debi White and indeed everyone who generously assisted along the way.

Malcolm Birkitt

Left, above and overleaf
Though the classic two-door Ford Thunderbird only enjoyed a production run of twelve years, three fundamentally different designs were created in that period. Of relatively compact proportions compared to later cars with the T-Bird appellation, are a 1957 Littlebird, a 1960 Squarebird and a 1963 Bigbird

The Birth of a Legend

Life begins at forty, or so they say. In which case, all the things that have happened to the Ford Thunderbird in its eventful thirty-odd year production run must be a precursor of something quite extraordinary yet to come. Time will tell.

The story of the Thunderbird car has its roots in post-war America, where the Ford Motor Co was struggling to extricate itself from one of those directionless troughs that every auto manufacturer experiences at some stage. New managerial blood was introduced in the latter half of the 1940s, to begin the process of resurrecting the company's fortunes.

At about the same time as this rehabilitation was taking place, returning US GIs were eulogizing about the smaller, agile sports cars produced in Britain – Triumphs, MGs, Austin Healeys and even the more luxurious Jaguars. In contrast to the bloated saloons seen on US highways, these vehicles were simply great fun to drive.

As the trickle of British sports cars exported across the Atlantic started to turn into a steady flow, more and more Americans began to fancy the idea of ownership. With a new sense of freedom and prosperity dawning, it seemed the USA was ready for a home-produced sports car too. Ford no doubt were thinking along these lines.

As it was, events quickly forced Ford's hand. Their arch rival – Chevrolet – launched the Corvette in late 1952. A sleek two-seat sportster of handsome proportions and excellent performance, it perfectly captured the mood of the moment and sent Ford scurrying off to the drawing board. A crash programme to design a 'personal' car was rapidly instigated – Ford executives didn't favour the conventional 'sports car' terminology. By early 1954, the project was virtually complete, thanks to hefty raiding of the existing parts bin – extensive retooling costs time as well as money. All it needed to commence production was an imaginative model name for the public to aspire to.

Like all good legends, the circumstances surrounding the adoption of the now revered 'Thunderbird' appellation are probably equal parts truth, gossip and imagination. Ford's advertising agency had come up with such scintillating gems as Beaver, Flag Liner, Hep Cat and Wheelaway. None of these were thought quite to capture either the spirit of the new car or the public's imagination. Another senior Ford executive forwarded the term 'Savile' – that didn't suit either.

Then, in response to a competition for the name – prize a $250 suit of clothes offered by the same executive – one of Ford's own stylists came up with 'Thunderbird'. A revered god from America's Southwest Indian culture, the soaring bird with talons hurling bolts of lightning was thought to bring rain and prosperity. As such it occupied that prestigious place right at the very top of the totem pole – a perfect motif for Ford. From that moment, they employed one very well dressed stylist and had found a title for the car which was to raise the heartbeat of America.

Legend has it that the emotive Thunderbird title was suggested by one of Ford's own stylists, after other curious suggestions had been discarded. Worshipped by America's Southwest Indians, this soaring bird from the very top of the totem pole was revered as a bringer of rain and prosperity. It certainly delivered the latter for the Dearborn company, as the T-Bird immediately outsold the rival Chevrolet Corvette by quite a huge margin

The Thunderbird lives on . . . in music videos or mock-period adverts, perched atop plinths as an advertising gimmick, or even selling pizzas. Cars never die, they're just recycled

After two decades of generally unconvincing design, Ford once again produced a car worthy of the Thunderbird name in 1989. It had a graceful shape, and two doors like the cars from the classic years of 1955–66, but only a fraction of their individuality

Compared to the bulbous American automotive designs of the late '40s and early '50s, the low, sleek profile of the first Thunderbird was a revelation. Cars like this 1956 example, with a roof height a whole foot lower than conventional Ford sedans, gave buyers a blend of European styling and American luxury and convenience

Littlebird ready to fly: 1955–57

Officially launched on October 22, 1954, as a 1955 model, Ford's rapidly cobbled-together response to the Corvette was an immediate success. Chevrolet had initially given their sports model a six-cylinder powerplant under its fibreglass bonnet. It had an ill-fitting manually operated soft-top and came with few of the luxury touches American buyers were accustomed to.

The first Thunderbird to appear on the showroom floor was also a sleek two-seater, but with less overt sporting pretensions. Instead, Ford aimed for a true performance car, but not at the expense of comfort. So proper roll-up side windows were featured, along with a choice of convertible or hard tops. There was something of a surprise hidden under the bonnet too.

Though beaten to the punch by Chevrolet, Ford weren't above displays of one-upmanship, aceing the Chevy's six-pot mill by placing a lusty V-8 under the bonnet of the Littlebird's steel body. Capacity was 292cid/4785cc, giving a respectable 0–60mph acceleration of around 11 seconds. The car had coil spring suspension up front, with a solid axle on leaf springs looking after the rear.

Just as the equipment package was well gauged, Ford scored a bullseye with the car's proportions. Clean, simple yet stylish lines were adopted, with a long bonnet sweeping up past the cabin to a short boot or trunk. The overall effect on a 102in wheelbase was rather elegant. In its first year, this combination of distinctive good looks, power and convenience enabled Ford to sell 16,000 units, heavily outstripping sales of the rival Corvette. Now it was Chevrolet's turn to go racing back to the drawing board.

Changes for the T-Bird's 1956 model year were few, emphasizing how the car's design team had got things right at the model's inception and illustrating that Detroit was unwilling to meddle with success. However, the 12-volt electrical system replaced the earlier 6-volt set-up, while the rear tyre was carried externally to improve available luggage space. Overall the '56 car weighed some 350 pounds more than the first model, and the outboard spare shifted weight distribution further toward the rear, making the car squat even more when accelerating – not a welcome trait.

Also, for the 1956 model the famous 'porthole window' top was offered to improve threequarter visibility – the '55 car had a bad blind spot at this point. Portholes were favoured by buyers four to one against the plain top. In fact, even with the porthole, visibility standards still had scope for improvement. In addition, a larger 312 cid/5112cc engine was offered as an option, enabling the car to accelerate as hard as earlier, lighter versions. Again, almost 16,000 Littlebirds were sold that year.

1957 Littlebird

Just 20 months from green light to production – that was Ford's cracking response to the Corvette. For its first year of production, the Thunderbird sported a relatively simple front fender arrangement with small indicator lights above. This is an early '55 model with chrome headlight bezels. Launch price was a modest $2,695 base, though most owners had various factory options fitted – power steering, electric windows, air conditioning. Both manual and automatic versions were offered

For 1957 Ford's two-seater underwent a minor facelift, with a revised front bumper/grille treatment. To the rear more pronounced fins, new taillights and an elongated boot were noticeable – the latter revision made necessary because American owners wanted space for both a set of golf clubs and the internally-carried spare tyre. A further refinement – some would call it a gimmick – was automatic volume control for the radio. The volume varied with the car's speed, enabling the driver to avoid deafening himself, passengers and by-standers at every traffic stop. Engine power was again upped, though displacement remained at 312 cu in/5112cc.

Sales of the much admired Thunderbird continued to climb – at the end of the 1957 year more than 21,000 were snapped up by the public. But a big shock for fans of the neat two-seat model was just around the corner. Ford management had decided that the car's sales volume must be substantially increased. So after just three full years, in which around 40,000 cars had been made, production was halted in favour of an altogether larger four-seat design. Sadly for some, the Littlebird had fallen to ground. But its replacement – the Squarebird – was ready for take off.

With its long raking bonnet, chrome dummy vents and V-8 badges, the 1955 T-Bird was hard to miss. Power output was 5 bhp higher in the automatic, to provide similar performance to the manual car

For 1956, Ford options included the famous 'porthole' hardtop, while the exterior mount spare tyre was standard issue to provide greater boot capacity. But the extra weight on the rear overhang brought handling problems, so the feature was deleted in the following model year

Above
Ford never intended the T-Bird to be a raw-boned sportster like the first Corvette. As can be seen from this 1957 car's interior, the accent was heavily on comfort, with six-way power seats, roll-up windows and a tachometer

Overleaf
1956 and '57 Littlebirds compared. For its final model year (on the left) Ford's personal car featured revised frontal treatment, with a more complex fender following the grille contour and incorporating rectangular indicators

Several companies in the USA cater solely for Thunderbird restoration and servicing. This is Jack Barnes' T-Bird shop in Houston, Texas, with a fine 1957 model just about prepared for the road again

In the 1957 design, the integral exhaust outlets moved to the extremities of the re-shaped rear fender

A series of Thunderbird logos were even incorporated into the door trim of the 1957 model. The porthole helped alleviate the claustrophobia some felt inside the car, and improved rearward visibility

Hard at work on a renovated V-8 motor for a 1957 T-Bird, at Lance Herrington's Thunderbird Southwest premises in Texas. Engine capacity for this model year was either 292 cid/4785 cc or 312 cid/5112 cc, giving 212 and 245 bhp respectively

For the more ostentatious Thunderbird driver, a lemon yellow paint scheme with a white porthole hardtop was guaranteed to turn heads. Even the wheels wore colour co-ordinated bands to set off the chrome hubcap from the whitewall tyres

*T-Bird Parking Only! Six immaculate
cars form the collection of Ray Smith,
a builder near Houston in Texas. They
include a quintet of Littlebirds and a
superb Monaco Limited Edition model*

Elegant in all-white, the proportions of this 1957 Littlebird still enjoy an integrity nearly four decades after the car's introduction. Wheelbase of the '55–'57 cars remained at 102 inches

For 1957, the Littlebird body
underwent mild restyling, with
splayed rear fins starting around the
door handle and a revised bumper
below the boot. The petrol filler cap
was relocated from the boot interior to
the offside. Note the small breeze
deflectors to keep hairstyles intact

Right
Ford liked T-Bird owners to remember what they were driving, so reminders proliferated around the car. Even the upholstery of this 1957 example carries the Thunderbird emblem in the vertical panel between the seats

Below
Raising the soft-top of the two-seat Littlebird is a laborious procedure, with various covers to move and replace. Not recommended if rain is imminent, or you haven't been practising at home and there's no friend to help

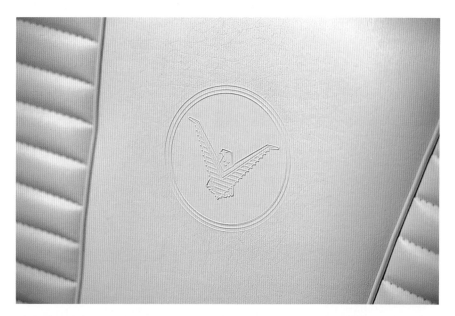

Above
Later Littlebirds still featured a single hooded binnacle over the instrument panel, but the speedometer had reverted to the traditional dial shape, with four smaller gauges clustered around. On this '57 model, an air-conditioning unit hangs below the dashboard over the transmission tunnel

Left
Ford's 312 cid/5112 cc V-8 unit is a rather snug fit under the Littlebird bonnet. Each bank of four cylinders carries a rocker cover with the T-Bird emblem cast in the fins, while the chrome air cleaner cover hides a four-barrel carburettor

Previous page
Underneath the slightly modified and 5-in-longer sheetmetal, the '57 T-Bird had a number of mechanical enhancements including beefier brakes, and a new rear axle. Power output was also up, with the hottest non-supercharged cars making 285 bhp thanks to a higher compression ratio and twin carbs

Right
Porthole hardtops outsold the plain version by four to one. Rear vision still wasn't wonderful, as the large blind spot was only partially removed, but people bought them simply because they looked good

Left
A power dome air-scoop on the bonnet added to the racy image and became a T-Bird trademark. It had a practical function, feeding air to the carburettor perched atop the inlet manifold

Below
Over 21,000 units saw the light of day in 1957, making this the most popular Littlebird by a good margin. Despite that success, the axe was just about to fall . . .

Though it looked fine from a distance, at close quarters this 1957 Florida Littlebird needed plenty of cosmetic restoration. Yet the owner was still asking $24,000 for the privilege of ownership in 1991

A T-Bird in the Family – Squarebird: 1958–60

Clearly, sentiment could play little part in the hard-headed automotive business of the mid-Fifties, especially at Ford. With greater volume in mind, development work on a bigger four-seat T-Bird had started in early 1955, barely six months after the two-seat car first rolled off the production line.

When the new design was revealed, those fond of Ford's first T-Bird may well have shaken their heads in disbelief. Though four headlights were deployed instead of two, 1958's version exhibited a frontal resemblance to the '57 car, but that, along with the Thunderbird name, was about the sum of their likenesses. The new model was significantly larger in most departments, and with it Ford had moved completely away from the sports theme and into the prestige marketplace.

Replacing the X-frame chassis of the '55–'57 car was a rigid unitized construction, with the wheelbase growing almost a foot to 113 inches. Similarly, length was increased by exactly 2 feet, and width by just over 4 inches. However, the absence of a separate chassis meant that just an inch was added to the car's height, so the new version still looked low and sleek with a 52.5 inch roofline. Coil spring suspension was employed throughout, with ball-joints at the front and trailing arms to the rear.

Apart from similarities around the nose, the 1958 model enjoyed a fresh appearance, yet one that was still essentially 'Thunderbird' in character. As before, add-on decoration was kept to a tasteful minimum, but body sculpting took on greater importance. This is particularly evident when the car is viewed from the side – one line swoops back from the headlamps and then curves down, linking with another feature which starts low in the door and continues to the rear bumper. It's possible that the need to strengthen bigger areas of sheet metal panelling account for these designs as much as aesthetic considerations, although it may be more charitable to view them as a happy marriage between design and technical considerations.

The car's interior suddenly seemed most spacious, partly because headroom had increased by one and a half inches, but the provision of a rear seat for the first time obviously radically changed the 'feel' of the interior. For the first time four occupants could travel in a T-Bird, opening up sales to the family man.

1960 Squarebird; the second generation

Ford's design team also excelled themselves in the way they handled entry into the rear of the car. This is never straightforward in a two-door layout, and the '58 T-Bird's low roofline didn't help matters either. The solution was huge doors, each just over four feet long and extending well past the folding front seats. As it turned out, exiting the car from the rear was easier than it was for front occupants, who had to negotiate a substantial windshield dog-leg!

Clever thinking was also apparent in another interior feature. A large transmission tunnel encroached into the available space, so rather than try to hide its bulk, Ford made a feature out of it with a stylish centre console. Grouped here were a radio, ash tray, heater controls and power window switches. Disadvantage turned to advantage, a sure sign of intelligent thinking in any field.

Curb weight of the new Squarebird at 3,869 pounds turned out to be only 429 pounds higher than the '57 two-seater – no T-Bird could ever be described as light, but this was less than many expected. Naturally, power output was increased correspondingly, with a 352 cu in/5768cc V-8 motor churning out exactly 300 horses and about 20% greater torque.

A spirited rather than sporty performance resulted, the automatic reaching 60mph from rest in around 10 seconds. But hard figures never give a full picture of a car's performance. Poor steering and cornering were typical complaints, especially from the experts. But with plenty of sound-deadening material giving a quiet ride, and the extra space and comfort available, the four-seat Thunderbird was an instant hit with American families. Ford's desire for increased volume was immediately realized with over 35,000 sales recorded.

Changes for 1959 (and for 1960) were rather limited, mainly because the T-Bird's development budget had been blown in the first year. An optional 430 cu in/7046cc 350hp V-8 motor reduced the 0–60mph time to just over 8 seconds, but nothing was done to improve the car's directional stability. Certain cosmetic changes percolated through, including a redesigned grille, side ornaments and new taillights.

Ford totally restyled the Thunderbird inside and out for the 1958 model year. Replacing the personal/sports car concept was a full four-seat prestige model, featuring unitary body construction. Overall height of the hardtop was just 1 in higher than its predecessor, but weight zoomed up 12%. Base price was $3630

The fussiness of the 1958 Squarebird nose contrasts with clean, streamlined front end of a '63 car

A completely automatic convertible hood model was available for 1960. At the touch of a button, the roof folded into the boot – very swish, even if carrying capacity was then reduced to virtually nothing. Three-speed manual plus overdrive or Cruise-O-Matic versions of the 352-engined car were also listed, plus a 350hp 430 cu in option in automatic only.

The 1959 and 1960 model years proved big sellers for the Squarebird, with 67,000 and 80,000 cars respectively registered in private ownership. Despite these excellent figures, Ford were once again looking at what the market required and about to spring another surprise in the Thunderbird story.

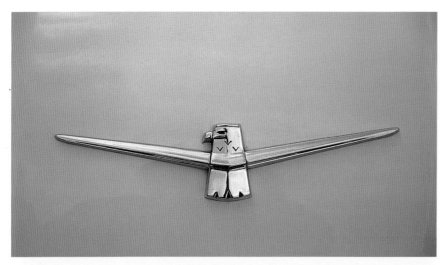

Left
One of numerous variations on the basic Thunderbird emblem, this time from a 1960 Squarebird

Below
As with the '56 car, Ford offered a continental kit option on the Squarebird for storage of the spare tyre outside the boot

THE DISTINGUISHED 59 FORD
THUNDERBIRD

THE CAR *EVERYONE* WOULD LOVE TO OWN

The publicity material for the 1959 model show that both hardtop and convertible versions of the four seat Thunderbird were available. Raising and lowering the soft-top was fully automatic, but boot space was severely hampered as a result. Bright metal tips appeared on the side panel projectiles

FORD THUNDERBIRD '59

The car everyone would love to own!

Unlike the Littlebird's single headlights, all Squarebirds had pairs of lights under those distinctive eyebrows

Among the modest styling changes for '60 cars was the removal of the chrome tips to the body panel projectiles

Despite moderate directional stability and slow steering, a stock Squarebird like this one almost won a 500 mile race at Daytona! Not even the smaller two-seater managed such a feat

*Engine options – all V-8s naturally –
included a 300 bhp 352 cid/5768 cc
and a 350 bhp 430 cid/7046 cc, the
latter with a pre-heated carburettor
induction system*

*Other external cosmetic additions for
'60 included these triple styling sashes
on the rear panels*

Most Squarebird owners opted for the
convenience of Ford's quaintly titled
Cruise-O-Matic automatic gearbox,
though the larger engined car also had
the option of a three speed manual
plus overdrive

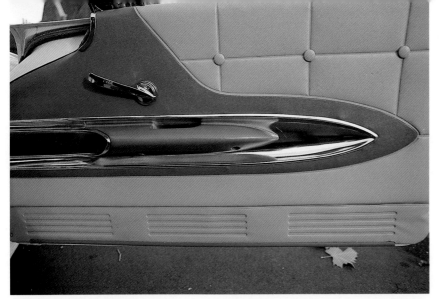

Left
Styling panache didn't stop with the outer panels on the Squarebird. Interior trim and furnishings, like this door detail, also showed a certain flair

Below
Dig those body panel shapes. Bomb flowing to rear starts near door hinge

Above
*Squarebird rear fins were splayed,
much as they had been on the two-seat
T-Bird*

Right
*Rocket-like triple rear light clusters
were set in complex surrounding
bumpers*

Above
The four seat Thunderbird had twin binnacles on the dashboard with a radio between. No attempts were made to disguise the large transmission tunnel, which apart from distancing driver from passenger, house window lifters, ashtray, radio speaker and ventilation controls. Bucket seats also hindered togetherness at the drive-in!

Right
Everything about the Squarebird was angular – even the door handles

The immense wrap-around windscreen on Squarebird projected into the entry/exit space, just as in the earlier Littlebird. Luckily the huge 4-feet plus doors allowed reasonably easy access to the car

Bigbird: 1961–63

Compared to the shock waves of 1958, which saw the Thunderbird concept transformed from a compact, sporty two-seater into a somewhat larger four-passenger cruiser, Ford's 1961 car spoke evolution rather than revolution. Though of similar size to the Squarebird – external dimensions were virtually identical – the third generation T-Bird came clothed in an entirely new, smoothly flowing body shape. Significant alterations were also noted in its unitised construction, the powerplant and in the interior design.

Clean, modern exterior lines – softer and less fussy than the earlier car – characterized this latest model. Headlamp pairs sat recessed in a neat tapered bonnet, the line of which climbed up and along the entire length of the body ending as a modest fin. At the rear, single round taillights sat integrated into the bumper design.

Hardtop and convertible models were again available, with the cabin length increased by a surprising 10 inches, despite the wheelbase remaining at 113in. Underneath the new sheetmetal, the unit body was welded up in two sections, and then joined at the cowl. This latter structure was lowered to give the '61 car better visibility than previous models.

Ease of entry and exit was much superior to either the Littlebird or the Squarebird, aided by even bigger doors and the elimination of the awkward dogleg windshield pillar. In addition, the new T-Bird had a novel feature – while the car was stationary, the steering wheel could be swung 10 inches to the right. Some may have thought this a gimmick, but long-legged drivers wouldn't agree.

Though the same ohv V-8 engine was used once more its displacement was upped, this time to 390 cu in/6384cc. Actual power output remained at 300 bhp, but torque was lifted by another 10 per cent, giving a 10.5 sec 0–60 mph time. No larger motor option was offered for 1961, and manual transmission was also deleted. But power-assisted steering and brakes became standard fitments.

With a much improved view from the cabin, more comfortable seating, superior instrumentation and many luxurious touches, the new T-Bird richly deserved its prestige tag. Its roadability was also significantly ahead of the Squarebird, with good braking and vastly better handling. Nimbler steering, reduced body roll while cornering and greater directional stability all helped dim the memory of the earlier model's vague responses. But handling still wasn't perfect. Suspension glitches continued to dog Ford, and insufficient damping meant keeping full control of the 4,110lb car proved as elusive as ever.

1962 Bigbird

The standard car received very minor changes for the next model year, limited to a reworked grille and fresh side trim. But 1962 also saw the launch of a special model, harking back to the glamorous two-seat era – the Sport Roadster. Its most obvious external feature was a stylish aerodynamic fibreglass tonneau covering the rear seats and providing swept-up headrests for front-seat passengers. Kelsey Hayes chromed wire wheels added to the 'performance' look.

Under the Sport Roadster's bonnet lurked a lusty 340 bhp version of the time-honoured V-8, the extra power generated by a high-compression 10.5:1 head breathing through triple carburettors. So the Sport T-Bird had superb looks, plenty of power and a flex-free body – very stiff for a convertible – but the general public weren't impressed. Sales were very poor and the car lasted just two model years. In contrast, the standard T-Bird sporting an attractive vinyl top and S-shaped Landau bars proved highly successful.

Yet another new grille saw the light of day for 1963, together with a styling crease on the front wings and doors. Once again, Ford had decided not to upset the applecart while the T-Bird was selling well. Instead, the big news of the year was made by yet another low volume model – the Limited Edition Landau. Launched in Monaco by the actress Grace Kelly, with an avalanche of razzamatazz and full Press attention, just 2,000 'Princess Grace' cars were built. Its elegant white paint scheme was set off by a rose vinyl top, while the interior had white leather upholstery and imitation rosewood trim. For a relatively modest outlay, the owner of a Landau could feel that he had staked his claim in the glamorous world of the international jetset.

Just three years after the introduction of the Squarebird, Ford once again heavily revised the T-Bird. This 1961 example shows completely new sheetmetal, hiding a series of mechanical improvements. Wheelbase remained at 113in, and 0–60mph was accomplished in 10.5 seconds

Previous page
Only marginal cosmetic differences were made between '62 and '63 – the later car had a toned down grille texture. These cars attended a Thunderbird convention in Houston, Texas

Right
For 1963, the Detroit stylists added a rather odd styling crease travelling down the wing and into the door

Most classic owners restore their cars to original or near condition, and the numbers of heavily doctored examples are few. This 1962 Florida T-Bird, for instance, wears a few mild customizing decals and dummy exhausts exiting forward of the rear wheels

Ford's long-lived ohv V-8 soldiered on in the Bigbird, its 390 cid/6390 cc producing 300 bhp as before but with torque increased by around 12 per cent

Above
The flowing '62 Thunderbird dashboard has a fixed steering wheel with auto shift stick at 2 'o clock. The manual gearbox option was no longer on the Ford list

Left
Chrome wire wheels are a late addition to this '62 model

Above
*Just like the earlier Squarebird,
chrome flashes appeared on the rear
quarter of the 1962 car*

Right
*Parked outside Lance Herrington's
specialist Thunderbird premises, the
clean lines of this 1962 Bigbird
convertible are very evident*

Ford simplified the rear-end treatment of their prestige car after the demise of the Squarebird, with large round lights and a plain bumper

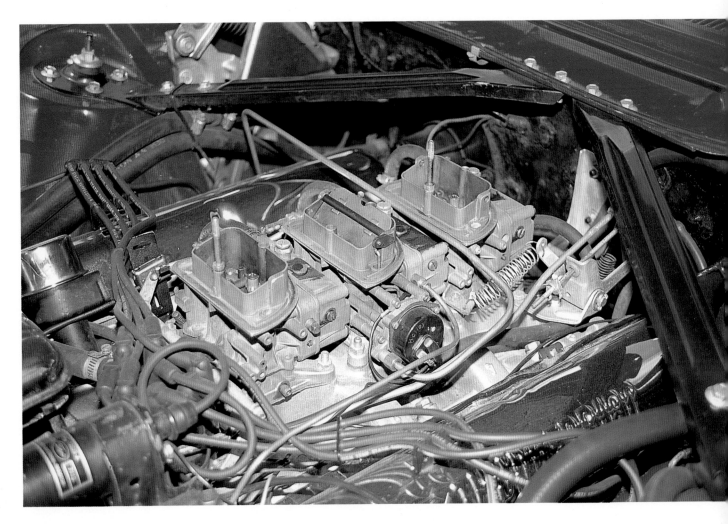

Above
Triple carbs gave the high-compression (10.5:1) M-series motor a hefty 340 bhp, but only a few hundred such cars were produced

Overleaf
With the hood up or down, the Bigbird soft-top must be one of the most pleasing cars to the eye that Ford have ever made. It was also one of the stiffest convertibles, thanks to the heavy unit construction body

Red interior of '63 Bigbird works a treat with chrome and machined metal trim

Left
A four headlamp treatment continued
with the Bigbird throughout its
'61–'66 production run. Any
resemblance to its British
contemporary the Ford Corsair
was purely intentional

Below
Front and rear overhangs are
considerable, but reversing
manoeuvres are aided by fins on wings
which reach the taillights

Right
Fiddling with small bits of chrome ornamentation was one of Ford styling department's less endearing characteristics

Below
The large transmission tunnel remained the dominant feature of T-Bird dashboard design. The four switches in the centre console are window lifters

Above
Larger, sunken taillights appeared for '62 and continued for the 1963 model year

Left
Wire wheels aided ventilation for the hard-worked front drums – brake fade was a recurring problem for the 4,000 pound plus T-Bird

Above
One spin-off from mainstream T-Bird production for 1963 included this Limited Edition Landau, the 'Princess Grace'. Just 2,000 cars were built

Right
The rose-coloured vinyl Landau roof distinguishes the Limited Edition car from run-of-the-mill T-Birds.

Above
The Monaco car's interior has luxurious white leather upholstery, and instead of the usual bright metal trim, fake rosewood applied to the dash, console and doors

Left
Press scribes of the time were flown to the Principality of Monaco for the Thunderbird launch, conducted for Ford by Princess Grace herself – the actress Grace Kelly. A commemorative numbered plate was attached to the centre console in each car

Bigbird hits middle age?
1964–66

Mechanically, Detroit's 1964 Thunderbird was virtually untouched, but the body featured considerable panel reshaping. With subtle curves replaced by assorted planes and angles, many people noted a distinct Squarebird feel to the new look. Ford emphatically denied they were turning back the clock, but the resemblance was pretty apparent. Typical was the redefined front end, the squaring off of the roof and the absence of fins around the boot. New thin rectangular stop/turn lights were also present, with a small Thunderbird motif in the centre of each strip.

Flow-through ventilation was the sole engineering innovation that model year. Boot capacity was marginally increased, though on the convertible the space was still completely filled by the folded hood. Rear occupants now relaxed in a classy, wrap-around seat. Despite earlier sales failures, a Sport Roadster option was also listed on the convertible.

Apart from assorted removal and addition of chrome decoration, the 1965 model year saw little external change. But one major mechanical step forward had been taken at last. The T-Bird became the first Ford to feature disc brakes as standard – about time, since the car's weight had climbed to a flabby 4700lbs and brake fade had become a serious problem with the drums fitted before. Discs reduced the chance of driving enjoyment coming to an abrupt and unpleasant halt. Sequential turn signals were also featured at the rear. The inner lamp came on first, then the second, and finally the outer, to indicate the driver's intentions.

The following year, 1966 brought the last of the compact two-door body shapes. Chief modifications for this model included the obligatory grille insert revamp and a flat, blade-like bumper to clean up the frontal treatment. Rear light clusters were now contained in a full width design, with the T-Bird badge placed slap in the middle.

Although the car had plenty of performance, via its 315 bhp V-8 of 390 cu in/6384 cc, the overall visual effect was one of blandness. Compared to the sculpture of the Squarebird and the sleek lines of the first Bigbird, the '66 car's anonymity created few sparks of electricity.

After twelve years of successful production, the T-Bird's youthful zest was over. The very first Thunderbird had been Ford's unabashed response to the sporty Chevrolet Corvette. Ten years later, American appetites were demanding bigger and ever more luxurious cars, and models from Buick and Oldsmobile were taking that market. Ford were determined that the Thunderbird should also fulfil that role. The first four-door T-Bird was just around the corner . . .

Bigbird 1965

Though mechanically unchanged, Ford's 1964 T-Bird made a curious styling U-turn. Its appearance harked back to the earlier Squarebird look

Despite poor sales on its debut in 1962, and the following year, the Sports Roadster returned in '64 for another market assault

Right

How do you turn a car with four seats into a stylish two-seater? Ford's marketing people had the answer — by placing a streamlined cover over the rear. At least it gave the T-Bird some covered storage space, useful since the boot was full of the folded down hood!

Below

Though its performance credentials were dubious, the Sports Roadster certainly looked the part from any angle (when standing still)

Plain side panel graphics are lifted by
Kelsey Hayes chrome wire wheels

Previous page
At the rear, the old jet rocket lights were now a distant memory. T-Bird motifs were inset into each rectangular light cluster. Boot capacity was increased to 11.5 cubic feet for '64, but the convertible still took up all of it!

Right
A 1965 T-Bird owned by Ron Gallops of Tampa, Florida

Left
Ford were forever shuffling the chrome trim on the T-Bird – here's yet another version of the car's motif

Below
Bigbird had a redesigned dashboard, including aircraft-type lever controls for air distribution and for the windscreen wipers

Above
Catch the right light, and the full intent of the body styling department is apparent

Right
The raising or lowering of the automatic soft-top of a T-Bird is still an awesome sight

Above
Look, no fins! Later classic T-Birds
eschewed such outdated styling
devices

Left
The boot lock of the '65 model lived
behind a sprung flap. This item was
prone to fall off when worn, and is
often missing

Even with clear echoes of late '50s Squarebird styling, the 1965 convertible could still turn friends green with envy

Classic T-Bird owners are expected to know where to buy the best chrome cleaner

A swingaway steering wheel was first
introduced in 1961, to aid access and
exit. Bigbird dashboard layout
employed a linear speedo above four
pod gauges

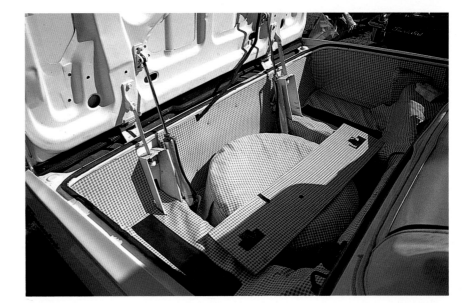

Right
The spare wheel of a 1965 convertible lived in the recess in the boot base, under the folding soft-top

Below
Disc brakes finally appeared for 1965, alleviating the fade problems which seriously affected earlier models. But that meant the attractive Kelsey Hayes wires didn't fit anymore

Rear wheel valances emphasized the long, low look

*An unusual green Bigbird Landau
owned by Don and Debi White of
Lutz, Florida*

*Like the convertible, '65 hardtop cars
also had divided rear accommodation*

Landau models sported distinguishing
S-irons on the rear pillars

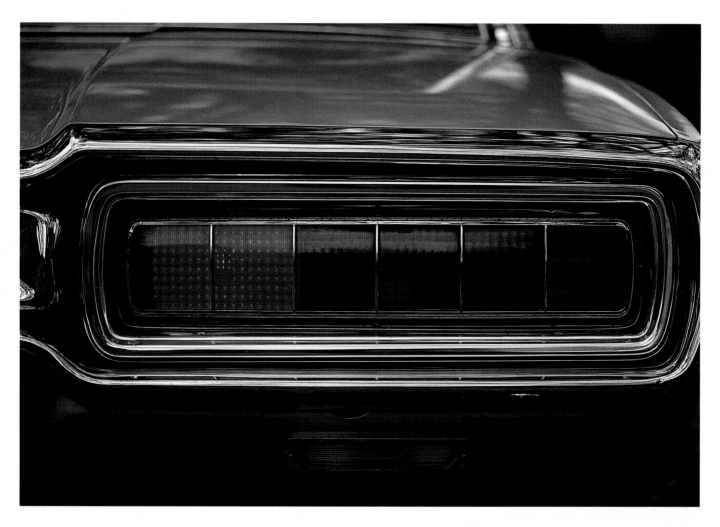

Sequential turn signals appeared for 1965, illuminating first the inner, then two and finally all three lamps to show the drivers' intentions

With more efficient disc brakes fitted, later classic T-Birds had no need of vented wheel covers

Left
Two and a half tons of T-Bird at speed is an impressive sight. Stopping the 4,700lb Bigbird proved less hair-raising once disc brakes were introduced in 1965

Above
Ford celebrated the extra stopping power of the '65 T-Bird by inscribing DISC BRAKE on the pedal itself! The small winder on the door operated the quarterlight

Ford personnel were too busy with the Mustang model to change the T-Bird much for the '65 model year

Previous page
*Although many questioned the later
Bigbird's styling, few could argue with
its popularity — almost 170,000 cars
were sold in 1964 and 1965*

Below
*An outboard 'continental' rear tyre
was a $900 aftermarket accessory
added to this '65 car some time in the
late 1980s*

Above
A replica tonneau cover reflects the looks of the earlier Sport Roadster

Overleaf
Bigbirds congregate in the rain at Houston

Previous page
Despite the fact that the last T-Bird covered in this volume rolled off the assembly line well over a quarter of a century ago, interest in the cars could hardly be greater. Of the 52,000 Littlebirds, 194,000 Squarebirds and 430,000 Bigbirds manufactured by Ford, a high percentage remain intact to support a thriving classic scene. Pictured is one of the last of the compact T-Birds produced in 1966

Right
For the first time in 1966, Ford allowed the T-Bird an area of painted metal below the front bumper

Note the slimline front bumper, large T-Bird motif in the grille and vestigial power dome on the bonnet which distinguish this '66 car. A sober enough looking machine

Despite its bland exterior, genuine power lurked under the bonnet of the 1966 T-Bird. The standard 390 cid/6384 cc V-8 was rated at 315 bhp, with a 428 cid/7014 cc monster developing 345 bhp on the option list

Above and right
*The interior of the '66 model
showed only detail differences to
the upholstery*

Previous page
If ever you get an opportunity to visit a T-Bird rally, take it – a friendlier bunch of people you won't meet

Right
It's in the blood. Many Americans who drove a T-Bird in the '50s and '60s have returned to ownership and restored one of these classics

Left and below
*A visit to one or the bigger T-Bird
gatherings offers an opportunity to
check out details on individual models.
Most owners seem to know the history
of their own car better than they do
that of their own family. At some of
the larger gatherings, there are more
gleaming, restored T-Birds than the
senses can take*

Membership of the largest classic
T-Bird club – the Vintage Thunderbird
Club International – has spilled over
into Australia and the UK. This is the
first ever display of the British chapter
at Newark in 1990